CARING FOR YOUR MENTAL HEALTH

Nurturing Your Mental Health in Today's World - Healing from Within, A Mindful Living and A Path to Mental Clarity and Balance

Dr. Martin Dosh

ISBN: 9798325659652
Imprint: Independently published

Cover design by: Art Painter Librar Congress Control Number: 2018675309

Printed in the United States of America

DEDICATION

To all those who dare to prioritize their mental well-being, this book is dedicated to you. In the journey of life, amidst its twists and turns, may these pages serve as a beacon of hope and guidance, May you find solace, strength, and inspiration within these words as you embark on the path of emotional self-care,

Your courage to nurture your mental health is a testament to resilience and self-love. May this book be a companion on your journey towards inner peace and wholeness,

With heartfelt gratitude.

Contents

INTRODUCTION

Caring for your mental health.

Taking care of your mental health is an essential part of your overall well-being. Emotional self-care involves prioritizing your emotional needs so that you can maintain a positive outlook and deal effectively with life's challenges. It's about creating a safe space for yourself in which you can feel, process your emotions, and take actions that support your mental health. In this book, we'll explore different ways to practice *emotional self-care and why it's important.*

CHAPTER ONE

Acknowledge your emotions

One of the most important steps in *emotional self-care* is acknowledging your emotions. It is important to recognize that all emotions are valid and that you have the right to feel them. Whether you feel sad, angry, anxious or happy, it is important that you allow yourself to feel your emotions fully. This means taking the time to reflect on your emotions, identify them, and understand why you feel them. Acknowledging your emotions can help you take steps to address them and care for yourself.

Practice self-compassion

Self-compassion involves treating yourself with the same kindness and understanding that you would extend to a good friend. It's about recognizing that everyone makes mistakes and that it's okay to be imperfect. Practicing self-compassion can reduce feelings of shame and self-criticism, which can negatively impact *your mental health*. One way to practice self-compassion is to talk to yourself in *a kind and supportive way*. For example, you might say to yourself, "It's okay to make mistakes. I'm trying my best.'

Connect with others

Humans are social beings and *social connections* are essential for *good mental health*. Connecting with others can help you feel supported and validated, which can positively impact *your emotional well-being*. This may include spending time with friends and family, joining *a social group*, or volunteering in your community. When you connect with others, you are more likely to feel a sense of belonging and purpose, which can help you cope with stress and setbacks.

Practice mindfulness

Mindfulness means paying attention to the present moment without judgment. It's about being fully present in the here and now, rather than dwelling on the past or worrying about the future. Practicing mindfulness can reduce feelings of stress and anxiety and improve your overall well-being. One way to practice mindfulness is to focus on your breathing. Take a few *deep breaths* and notice the feeling of the air moving in and out of your body. If your mind wanders, gently bring your attention back to your breathing.

Seek *professional help*

If you are struggling with your mental health, it is important to seek professional help. Mental health professionals can provide you with the support and guidance you need to manage your emotions and cope with life's challenges. They can help you develop coping skills, identify negative thought patterns, and create a plan to improve your mental health . There are many different types of mental health professionals, including therapists, counselors, and psychiatrists. If you're not sure where to start, contact your doctor or a trusted friend or family member for a referral.

Emotional self-care is an essential part of overall well-being. By acknowledging your emotions, practicing self-compassion, connecting with others, practicing mindfulness, and seeking *professional help* when needed, you can create a safe space for yourself that supports *your mental health*. Remember that taking care of yourself is not selfish; it is necessary that you can fully show up in your life and be there for those you love.

CHAPTER TWO

The Ripple Effect of Compassion.

Compassion, a fundamental element of the *Human Life Approach*, is a quality that knows no bounds. It is a universal language that transcends cultural, religious and geographical boundaries. Compassion is not merely an isolated act of kindness; rather, it is an intricate web of *interconnectedness* that has a profound and far-reaching impact on individuals, communities and society as a whole. In this section, we explore the ripple effect of compassion, delving into its *transformative power* from multiple perspectives and highlighting *the countless ways* it enriches our lives.

Personal transformation:

Compassion starts at the individual level. When we cultivate compassion within ourselves, it transforms us on *a personal level.* By empathizing with others, we come into better contact with our own emotions and vulnerabilities. Compassion fuels emotional intelligence, leading to greater self-awareness, self-acceptance and resilience. It helps us grow as individuals and promotes a sense of *inner peace* and contentment. For example, someone who practices self-compassion is more likely to overcome self-criticism and build healthier self-esteem.

Improve relationships:

Compassion is the glue that binds us to our loved ones. When we show compassion to family, friends, and even strangers, we build stronger, *more meaningful relationships.* Acts of kindness, understanding and support create a foundation of trust and goodwill, resulting in more harmonious and lasting connections. Think about how a compassionate friend who listens without judgment can change your day, or how a compassionate partner can strengthen the bond between two people going through *difficult times.*

Community cohesion:

Compassion extends beyond the individual and into the community. When communities practice compassion, they become more inclusive and supportive. Neighbors help neighbors, and people unite to tackle common challenges. For example, a community coming together to help people affected by a natural disaster demonstrates the profound impact of *collective compassion.* Such solidarity can lead to *a resilient and close-knit community.*

Social change:

Compassion has the power to create social change and address systemic problems. When individuals and groups work together with empathy and compassion, they can advocate for justice, equality and human rights. The civil rights movement in the United States, led by figures such as Martin Luther King Jr., was driven by compassion for a more just and equal society. This compassion led to *groundbreaking changes* in the country's laws and *social norms.*

Global impact:

Compassion knows no bounds; it transcends cultural and geographical boundaries. The ripple effect of compassion is spreading globally, as acts of goodwill and support reach those in need around the world. Humanitarian organizations and volunteers around the world exemplify the transformative power of global compassion. Organizations like *Doctors without Borders* and the Red Cross provide health care and assistance to people in crisis, highlighting *the far-reaching impact* of global compassion.

Mental Health and Wellbeing:

Compassion is not only about the way we treat others, but also about the way we treat ourselves. Self-compassion is a crucial aspect of mental health and well-being. People who practice self-compassion are more resilient in the face of adversity, less prone to stress and anxiety, and *better equipped* to deal with life's challenges. Self-compassion acts as a buffer against negative self-talk and self-criticism and promotes *a more positive and nourishing inner dialogue.*

Compassion is a cornerstone of the *Human Life Approach*, and its ripple effect touches every aspect of our lives. From personal growth and stronger relationships to community unity, social change, global impact and improved *mental health*, compassion is a force that enriches and transforms us all. It reminds us that our actions, no matter how small, have the potential to create *profound and positive change in the world.*

CHAPTER THREE

The Negative Effects of Over thinking on Mental Health .

Over thinking is a common problem that many people suffer from, causing them to worry excessively and worry about things that are often out of their control. While it is normal to have some level of worry and anxiety, over thinking can be detrimental to a person's mental health and well-being. In this section, we explore the negative effects of over thinking on *mental health*.

1. Increased anxiety and stress levels

Over thinking can cause a person's anxiety and stress levels to skyrocket. When a person is constantly preoccupied with negative thoughts and worries, their body's stress response is activated, leading to the release of stress hormones such as cortical. Over time, this can lead to chronic stress and anxiety, which can negatively impact a person's physical and mental health.

2. Insomnia and sleep problems

Over thinking can also lead to insomnia and other sleep problems. When a person's mind is constantly occupied with worries and stress, it can be difficult to relax and fall asleep. This can lead to *a vicious cycle* of sleep deprivation, which can further exacerbate feelings of anxiety and stress.

3. Negative self-talk and *low self-esteem*

Over thinking can also lead to negative self-talk and low self-esteem. When a person constantly berates themselves with *negative thoughts* and worries, it can undermine their self-confidence and self-esteem. This can lead to feelings of depression and hopelessness, making it even more difficult to break the cycle of over thinking.

4. Difficulty focusing and making decisions

Over thinking can also make it difficult to concentrate and make decisions. When someone is constantly worrying and worrying, it can be difficult to focus on anything else. This can make it difficult to complete tasks, meet deadlines, and make *important decisions.*

5. Relationship problems

Over thinking can also cause problems in relationships. When someone constantly worries and worries, it can lead to misunderstandings, miscommunication, and *hurt feelings*. This can strain relationships with friends, family, and *romantic partners, making it even harder to break the cycle of over thinking.*

In general, over thinking can have a significant negative effect on a person's mental health and well-being. If you find yourself struggling with over thinking, there are several strategies you can try to break the cycle. These include mindfulness meditation, cognitive behavioral therapy, and self-care practices such as exercise and healthy eating. By taking steps to calm your mind and reduce your worries and fears, you can improve your mental health and enjoy *a more fulfilling life.*

CHAPTER FOUR

Prioritizing Self-Care and Mental Well-Being.

As we navigate through life, we inevitably face challenges and setbacks that can negatively impact our mental health. Resilience, the ability to recover from setbacks, is a key factor in maintaining our mental well-being. However, it is important to note that resilience is not just about persevering or persevering. It also means prioritizing self-care and taking proactive steps to protect our mental health.

Practice mindfulness and self-reflection

Mindfulness is the practice of being present in the moment and observing our thoughts and feelings without judgment without getting caught up in them. It can help us develop a greater sense of self-awareness and regulate our emotions. Self-reflection is also an important tool for building resilience. By reflecting on our experiences we can **identify our strengths and weaknesses** and learn from our mistakes.

Build healthy *habits*

Our physical and mental health is closely linked. Establishing healthy habits, such as regular exercise, a balanced diet, and good sleep hygiene, can go a long way in maintaining our mental well-being. Exercise in particular has numerous mental health benefits , including reducing symptoms of anxiety and depression.

Connect with others

Social support is another important factor in building resilience. connecting with others can provide emotional support, make us feel less alone, and give us a sense of belonging. It is important to build meaningful relationships with friends, family and community members.

Seek *professional help* when necessary

It is important to recognize when we need extra support and seek *professional help* if necessary. This may be therapy, medication or other forms of treatment. Seeking help is a sign of strength, not weakness, and can provide us with the tools we need to deal with life's challenges.

Practice self-compassion

Finally, it is important to practice self-compassion. This means treating ourselves with kindness, understanding, and forgiveness, rather than with self-criticism or judgment. Self-compassion can help us bounce back from setbacks and cultivate *a greater sense of resilience.*

Building resilience is not just about persevering or persevering. It also means prioritizing self-care and taking proactive steps to protect our mental health. By practicing mindfulness and self-reflection, developing healthy habits, connecting with others, seeking professional help when needed, and practicing self-compassion, we can cultivate greater resilience and maintain our mental well-being.

CHAPTER FIVE

The role of gratitude in mental health and well-being .

Gratitude is a powerful emotion that can have a significant impact on our mental health and well-being. It is the act of gratitude and appreciation for the people, things and experiences in our lives. When we practice gratitude, we shift our focus from what we lack to what we have, which can improve *our overall sense* of happiness and contentment.

Gratitude and positive thinking

Gratitude is closely linked to positive thinking, which is an essential aspect of *mental health*. When we focus on the positive aspects of our lives, we are more likely to feel hopeful, optimistic and happy. Gratitude can help us reframe *negative* experiences and find the positive in every situation. For example, if we experience a setback at work, we can focus on the lessons we learned from the experience and be grateful for the opportunity to grow and improve.

Gratitude and stress reduction

Stress is a common factor that can negatively impact our mental health and well-being. When we are stressed, our bodies release cortical, a hormone that can cause a range of physical and *mental health* problems. Gratitude can help reduce stress by promoting relaxation and reducing cortical production. When we focus on the things we are grateful for, we activate *the parasympathetic nervous system* , which is responsible for calming the body and reducing stress.

Gratitude and resilience

Resilience is the ability to recover from setbacks and overcome challenges. Gratitude can help build resilience by providing a positive perspective on life's challenges. When we are grateful, we are more likely to see obstacles as opportunities for growth and development. For example, when we experience a setback in *our personal relationships*, we can be grateful for the people who support us and for the lessons we learn about ourselves and others.

Gratitude and relationships

Gratitude can also improve our relationships with others. When we express gratitude to the people in our lives, we strengthen our connections and build trust and intimacy. Gratitude can also help us forgive and let go of resentments, which can improve our relationships with others. For example, if we have a disagreement with a friend, expressing gratitude for their support and understanding can help us overcome the conflict and strengthen our bond.

Gratitude and self-care

Self-care is an essential aspect of mental health and well-being. Gratitude can help us prioritize self-care by reminding us of the things that bring us joy and fulfillment. When we are grateful, we are more likely to engage in activities that nourish our bodies and minds, such as exercise, meditation, and spending time with loved ones. Gratitude can also help us recognize when we need to take a break and prioritize our mental and emotional health.

Overall, cultivating gratitude is an effective way to improve our mental health and well-being. By focusing on *the positive aspects* of our lives we can reduce stress, build resilience, improve our relationships and prioritize self-care. Whether we express our gratitude by journaling, meditating, or simply saying thanks, the benefits of gratitude are clear. So let's take a moment to appreciate the people, things, and experiences that make our lives meaningful and fulfilling.

CHAPTER SIX

Laughter as a tool for dealing with setbacks and trauma .

Adversity and trauma are inevitable parts of life and can be difficult to deal with. However, laughter can be a powerful tool in dealing with these challenges. Laughter has been shown to have numerous physical and mental health benefits, and can help people feel better and cope with *difficult situations*. In this section we explore the ways in which laughter can be used as a tool for coping with adversity and trauma.

Laughter can reduce stress and anxiety

When we face adversity or trauma, it is normal to feel stressed and anxious. However, laughter can help reduce these feelings. When we laugh, our bodies release endorphins, which are natural feel-good chemicals that can help reduce stress and anxiety. Additionally, laughter can help lower the levels of stress hormones in the body, which can help lower blood pressure and improve *overall health*.

Laughter can improve mood and mental health

In addition to reducing stress and anxiety, laughter can also improve mood and *mental health*. When we laugh, our brains release dopamine, a neurotransmitter associated with pleasure and reward. This can help us feel happier and more positive, even in the face of setbacks. Additionally, laughter has been shown to have a positive effect on *mental health*, reducing symptoms of depression and anxiety.

Laughter can improve relationships

When we laugh with others, it can help strengthen our relationships. Laughter can create a sense of connection and camaraderie, and it can help break down barriers and build trust. Additionally, laughter can help reduce tension and conflict, making it easier to resolve disagreements and communicate effectively.

Humor can help reframe *difficult situations*

Humor can be a powerful tool for reframing *difficult situations*. If we can find humor in a difficult situation, it can help us see things from a different perspective and find new solutions to problems. Additionally, humor can help reduce the intensity of negative emotions, making it easier to deal with *challenging situations*.

Laughter can be a form of self-care

Laughter can also be a form of self-care. Taking time to laugh and enjoy ourselves can help us recharge and reduce feelings of burnout and exhaustion. Furthermore, laughter can be a way to cope with the stress and uncertainty of *everyday life*, making us feel more resilient and better able to cope with whatever comes our way.

Laughter can be a powerful tool in dealing with adversity and trauma. It can reduce stress and anxiety, improve mood and mental health, strengthen relationships, help reframe *difficult situations* and be a form of self-care. By integrating laughter into our lives, we can improve *our overall well-being* and better cope with the challenges that come our way.

CHAPTER SEVEN

Prioritizing Self-Care and Well-Being .

Mindful goal setting is a crucial aspect of prioritizing self-care and well-being. It's essential to take the time to think about what we want to achieve and what serves our highest good. It's easy to get caught up in the hustle and bustle of everyday life and forgetting to take care of ourselves. However, if we don't take care of ourselves, we can't be our best selves for others. That's why it's crucial to prioritize self-care and wellness when setting goals.

Set realistic goals:

When setting goals, it is essential to set realistic goals that are achievable. Setting unrealistic goals can lead to disappointment and frustration, which can be detrimental to our well-being. It is important to set goals that are challenging but achievable. For example, if you want to start exercising, start with a few days a week instead of every day.

Prioritize Self-Care:

Self-care should be a top priority when setting goals. It is essential to take care of ourselves physically, mentally, and emotionally. This can include things like getting enough sleep, eating *healthy foods*, exercising, and taking time for ourselves to to relax and recharge.

Take Your Mental Health Into Consideration:

Mental health should be a top priority when setting goals. It is essential to take care of our mental health by practicing mindfulness, seeking therapy when necessary, and taking breaks when necessary. We must be aware of our *mental health* and take *the necessary steps* to maintain it.

Practice Gratitude:

Practicing gratitude is an excellent way to prioritize self-care and wellness. Taking time to think about what we are grateful for can help us shift our focus from negativity to positivity. It can also help us help us appreciate *the good things in our lives, which can lead to greater happiness and well-being.*

Be Flexible:

It is essential to be flexible when setting goals. Life can be unpredictable and sometimes things don't go as planned. It is crucial to be open to change and adjust our goals when necessary. Being flexible can help us avoid disappointment and frustration and can lead to greater well-being.

Mindful goal setting is an essential aspect of prioritizing self-care and wellness. It is crucial to set *realistic goals*, prioritize self-care, consider our *mental health*, practice gratitude, and be flexible. By doing this, we can achieve our goals while also taking care of ourselves and promoting *our overall well-being*.

CHAPTER EIGHT

The role of creative expression in mental health.

Creative expression can have a powerful impact on mental health. The process of creating art, whether it is painting, drawing, writing, or any other form of expression, can serve as a therapeutic outlet for those struggling with mental illness. Many mental health professionals include art therapy in their treatment plans. By engaging in *creative expression,* individuals can explore their emotions, reduce stress, and gain a sense of control over their thoughts and feelings.

Here are a few ways *creative expression* can positively impact *mental health*:

1. *Emotional Expression:*

Creating art can be a way to express emotions that may be difficult to put into words. For example, someone struggling with depression may find it difficult to put their feelings into words, but painting or drawing may help them convey their emotions more easily.

2. Stress Relief: Engaging in creative activities can be a great way to reduce stress and anxiety. The act of creating can be meditative and help calm the mind.

3. *Improved Self-Esteem*: Creating something can give individuals a sense of satisfaction and pride. This can be especially helpful for people who struggle with *low self-esteem.*

4. Sense of control: Mental illness can often make people feel like they have no control over their thoughts or emotions. By participating in *creative activities*, individuals can gain a sense of control over their own experiences.

5. Community Building: Participating in art classes or groups can give individuals a sense of community and connection . This can be especially important for those who feel isolated due to *their mental health problems.*

For example, Tila, *a young artist*, started painting as a way to cope with her fears. She found that the process of creating allowed her to focus on something other than her worries, and that painting was soothing and meditative. Painting allowed Tila to express her emotions in a way that felt safe and non-judgmental. Over time, Tila's art became a source of pride and achievement, which helped boost her self-esteem. Additionally, Tila started taking art classes and found that the sense of community she gained from being around other artists was incredibly beneficial to her mental health.

CHAPTER NINE

Prioritizing Healthy Attachment for Better Mental Health.

When it comes to *mental health*, there are many factors that contribute to our overall well-being. One of the most important of these factors is our attachment style. Our attachment style is the way we connect and bond with others, and plays an important role in shaping our emotional and psychological development. In this section, we explore the importance of prioritizing healthy attachment for better *mental health*.

1. The impact of attachment on *mental health*

Research has shown that our attachment style has a significant impact on our *mental health*. Children who have secure bonds with their caregivers tend to have better emotional regulation, higher self-esteem, and *stronger social skills*. On the other hand, children with *insecure attachments*, such as avoidant or anxious attachment styles, are more likely to suffer from *psychological problems* such as anxiety and depression. These patterns can continue into adulthood, affecting our relationships and our overall well-being.

2. The importance of early intervention

Early intervention is crucial when it comes to promoting healthy attachment and preventing mental health problems. Parents and caregivers can play an important role in shaping a child's attachment style by providing a safe and nurturing environment. Therapy can also be helpful in addressing attachment issues and promoting healthy relationships.

3. The role of therapy in promoting *healthy attachment*

Therapy can be an effective way to promote healthy attachment and improve mental health. Various approaches, such as attachment-based therapy and cognitive behavioral therapy, can help individuals develop more secure attachment styles and improve their relationships with others. For example, attachment-based therapy focuses on creating a safe and nurturing therapeutic relationship that can serve as a model for *healthy attachment* in other areas of life.

4. The benefits of healthy attachment in adulthood

Developing a healthy attachment style in adulthood can have significant benefits for our mental health and overall well-being. Adults with secure attachments tend to have better emotional regulation, *stronger social skills,* and more satisfying relationships. They are also less likely to have *psychological problems* such as anxiety and depression.

5. **The importance of *ongoing support***

While early intervention is critical, ongoing support is also essential in promoting healthy attachment and improving mental health. This may include therapy, support groups, and other resources that can help individuals maintain healthy relationships and deal with challenges as they arise.

Prioritizing healthy attachment is essential for better *mental health.* By promoting secure attachments in childhood and adulthood, we can improve emotional regulation, social skills, and overall well-being. Early intervention and ongoing support are critical in promoting healthy attachment and preventing *mental health* problems. Therapeutic approaches such as attachment-based therapy can be effective in promoting *healthy attachment* and improving relationships.

CHAPTER TEN

The impact of debt on mental health.

Debt is a major source of stress for many people. It can be a burden that affects not only their financial well-being, but also their *mental health*. According to a study, people with debt are more likely to suffer from depression and anxiety. Debt can cause a feeling of helplessness and hopelessness, and it can lead to a loss of self-esteem. Debt can be a vicious cycle because the stress they cause can make it more difficult to pay off the debt. This creates *an endless cycle* of debt accumulation fatigue.

To understand the impact of debt on mental health, here are *some insights* from different points of view:

1. Debt can cause a feeling of shame and guilt. Individuals may feel ashamed of *their financial situation* and try to hide it from others. This can cause them to isolate from their friends and family, leading to feelings of loneliness and depression.

2. Debt can also cause a feeling of anxiety and stress. Individuals may worry about how they will pay off their debts, and this can cause them to lose sleep all the time and feel

anxious. This can lead to *physical health problems,* such as headaches and stomach aches.

3. Debt can lead to loss of control. Individuals may feel like they have lost control of their finances and their lives . This can lead to feelings of helplessness and hopelessness, which can lead to depression.

4. Debt can also affect relationships. Couples may argue about money, and individuals may feel like they are a burden to their loved ones. This can lead to feelings of resentment and anger, which can put a strain on relationships.

To break the cycle of debt accumulation fatigue, it is important to take action. Here are some steps individuals can take to improve their financial situation and mental health:

1. Make a budget and stick to it. This can help people **regain control of their finances** and reduce stress.

2. Seek help from *a financial advisor* or debt counselor. These professionals can provide guidance and support in paying off debt and managing finances.

3. Practice self-care. This may include exercise, meditation, or spending time with loved ones. Taking good care of yourself can improve mental health and reduce stress .

4. Focus on the positive. Instead of dwelling on the negative aspects of debt, focus on the progress being made in paying it off. Celebrate *small victories* along the way .

By taking these steps, individuals can break the cycle of debt accumulation fatigue and improve *their financial and mental well-being.*

CHAPTER ELEVEN

The psychological impact of shortage anxiety on consumers.

The fear of shortages is a real concern for consumers, especially in times of crisis, when the availability of goods and services becomes uncertain. This type of fear arises when consumers believe that they will not have access to the things they need or want in the future. It can lead to panic buying, hoarding, and other behaviors that worsen the problem. The psychological impact of deficiency anxiety is far-reaching and can affect people's *mental health* , well-being and *overall quality of life* .

There are several reasons why fear of shortages can have a significant psychological impact on consumers. First, uncertainty about the future can be very unsettling. When people don't know what to expect, they can feel anxious, stressed or even depressed. Second, the fear of missing out (FOMO) can be a powerful motivator. When consumers believe that others are buying up all available goods, they may feel a sense of urgency to do the same. Finally, scarcity can create a perception of value. When things are scarce, they can be perceived as more valuable than they really are, causing consumers to overvalue them and make *irrational purchasing decisions* .

To better understand the psychological impact of shortage anxiety on consumers, here are *some in-depth insights*:

1. **The fear of shortages can lead to panic buying and hoarding.** When consumers worry about shortages, they may panic buy or hoard to feel like they have more control. They can store goods and supplies even when they don't need them, to ensure they can access them in the future. This behavior can exacerbate the problem of shortages, making it even more difficult for others to access the goods they need.

2. **Fear of deficiency can have a negative effect on mental health and well-being.** If people worry about shortages, it can have a negative impact on their mental health and well-being. They may feel stressed, anxious or depressed, which can affect their ability to function in their daily lives. This can lead to a vicious cycle, where fear of deficiency leads to *poor mental health* , which in turn worsens anxiety.

3. **Fear of shortages can create a sense of community.** Fear of shortages can be a negative experience, but it can also create a sense of community among consumers. People can come together to share information and resources and support each other during *difficult times*. This sense of community can be a positive consequence of fear of shortages, making people feels more connected and less alone.

The fear of shortages is a real concern for consumers and can have significant psychological consequences. Consumers may engage in panic buying or hoarding, experience *negative mental health* impacts, or experience a sense of community during times of scarcity. By understanding the psychological impact of fear of shortages, consumers can be better equipped to deal with uncertainty in the marketplace.

CHAPTER TWELVE

The Importance of Understanding Behavioral Patterns.
Understanding behavioral patterns is crucial for anyone who wants to break negative cycles and improve quality of life. Behavioral patterns are the habits and routines that people develop over time, and they can be either positive or negative. Positive patterns can **help people achieve their goals**, while negative patterns can hold them back and cause problems in their personal and professional lives. In this section we explore the importance of understanding behavior patterns and how they can be changed.

1. *Understanding* the roots of behavioral patterns

Behavioral patterns are influenced by a variety of factors, including genetics, environment and personal experiences. Understanding the roots of behavioral patterns is essential to identify what causes negative patterns and how to change them. For example, someone who experienced trauma in childhood may develop negative behavior patterns that stem from their experiences. By understanding the root cause of these patterns, they can work to address the underlying issues and develop positive patterns.

2. **The impact of behavioral patterns on *mental health***

Behavioral patterns can have a significant impact on mental health. Negative patterns can lead to anxiety, depression and other mental health problems. For example, someone who has developed a pattern of negative self-talk may struggle with low self-esteem and feelings of worthlessness. By understanding the impact of behavioral patterns on mental health , individuals can work to develop *positive patterns* that promote *mental well-being* .

3. **Break negative behavioral patterns**

Breaking negative behavioral patterns can be a challenge, but with the right approach it is possible. One option is to seek professional help from a therapist or counselor who can help identify *negative patterns* and work to change them. Another option is to develop positive habits and routines that replace *negative patterns*. For example, someone who struggles with procrastination might develop a routine of breaking down tasks into *smaller, manageable steps* to break the pattern of putting things off.

4. **The importance of consistency**

Consistency is key when it comes to breaking behavioral patterns. It takes time and effort to develop new habits and routines, and it's essential to stick with them, even when it feels hard. Making small, consistent changes over time can lead to *significant improvements* in behavior patterns and *overall quality* of life.

5. **The benefits of positive behavior patterns**

Developing positive behavior patterns can have a number of benefits, including better mental health, increased productivity and better relationships. For example, someone who develops a pattern of regular exercise may experience improved physical and mental health, as well as increased energy and focus.

Understanding behavioral patterns is essential for anyone who wants to break negative cycles and improve quality of life. By identifying the root causes of *negative patterns*, seeking professional help, developing positive habits and routines, and staying consistent, individuals can break *negative behavior patterns* and reap the benefits of positive ones.

CHAPTER THIRTEEN

Take Your Mental Health Into Consideration.

Losing your job can be one of the most stressful experiences of your life. It can be overwhelming and cause you to feel a range of emotions, from sadness and fear to anger and despair. It is important to consider *your mental health* during this time and take care of yourself both emotionally and physically. Here are *some crucial steps* to surviving job loss:

Acknowledge your feelings.

It is normal to feel upset, scared and angry when you lose your job. Allow yourself to grieve the loss and try not to bottle up your emotions.

Talk to someone.

Talking to a trusted friend or family member can help you process your feelings and give you support. If you don't feel comfortable talking to someone you know, there are many free help lines available to help you, such as the Samaritans in the

UK (116 123) or the *National Suicide Prevention Lifeline* in the US
(1 -800-273-8255).

Stay active and healthy.

Exercising releases endorphins, which have a mood-boosting
effect, so try to stay active even when you don't feel like it.
Eating healthy and getting enough sleep are also important for
maintaining *your mental health*.

Make a plan.

Once you've had time to process your emotions, it's important
to think about what you want to do next. If you're not sure
what you want to do, there are many free online career advice
resources and services available to help you figure it out.

5. Take action. Once you have a plan, it's time to take action
and start working on your goals. This can be a challenging time,
but remember that it is also an opportunity for growth and
change.

CHAPTER FOURTEEN

Exploring the Benefits of FamTech Startups:Improving Mental Health and Well-Being:

Digital Support for Families.

Accessible resources for *mental health* care:

Digital support platforms can play a crucial role in improving mental health and well-being for families. These platforms provide easy access to a wide range of resources, such as online counseling services, *mental health* screening tools , and self-help guides. Apps such as TalkSpace and BetterHelp provide for example, virtual therapy sessions, which allow families to connect with licensed therapists from the comfort of their own home. This convenience can be especially helpful for *busy parents* who may find it difficult to make time for *in-person therapy appointments*.

Educational Resources for Parenting:

Digital platforms also provide a wealth of educational resources for parents, helping them navigate the challenges of raising children and promoting positive mental health outcomes. For example, websites such as Parenting.com and BabyCenter offer articles, videos, and forums where parents can learn about different parenting techniques, gain insight from experts and connect with other parents facing similar challenges. These resources can empower families to provide knowledge and support, improving their ability to promote *mental well-being* in their households to promote, to promote.

Gamified Mental Health Apps:

Engaging children in activities that promote mental well-being can be a challenge. However, gamified mental health apps offer an innovative solution to this problem. These apps combine entertainment with mental health exercises, making it easier for children and parents to enjoy activities businesses that promote emotional well-being. For example, apps like Smiling Mind and Mood Mission provide interactive games and exercises that help children manage stress, build resilience, and develop positive coping mechanisms. By incorporating fun and interactive elements , these apps can help *promote emotional well-being making support* more attractive and accessible to *the whole family* .

Online Support Groups:

Digital platforms facilitate connection and support through online communities and support groups. Families can find comfort by communicating with others going through similar challenges and providing a sense of connection and understanding. Platforms such as Facebook groups, Reddit communities and specialized forums provide spaces where families can share experiences, ask questions, and offer each other support. These online support groups can be especially helpful for families dealing with specific issues, such as raising a

Mindfulness and Meditation Apps:

In today's fast-paced world, finding moments of calm and practicing mindfulness can greatly benefit families' mental health. Mindfulness and meditation apps, such as Headspace and Calm, offer guided meditation exercises and relaxation techniques that can easily be incorporated into daily routines .Families can use these apps together to cultivate a sense of relaxation and well-being, reduce stress levels, and promote overall mental health .

In conclusion, digital support for families can play an important role in improving mental health and well-being . From accessible resources and educational tools to gamified apps and online support groups, these digital platforms provide families with convenient and engaging ways to **prioritize their mental**

health .By embracing these digital solutions , families can foster *a supportive and nurturing environment* that promotes the well-being of all its members.

CHAPTER FIVETEEN

Stories of resilience and empowerment.

Celebrating progress:

stories of resilience and empowerment

On the path to promoting mental health, it is critical to recognize and celebrate the progress made by individuals who have overcome challenges and emerged stronger. These stories of resilience and empowerment serve as beacons of hope, inspiring others to persevere and reminding us of the incredible power of the human spirit. By sharing these stories, we can foster a sense of community and support, break the stigma around *mental health, and encourage individuals* to seek help when they need it.

The power of *shared experiences*

One of the most powerful ways to promote resilience and empower individuals is by sharing *personal stories*. By listening to others who have faced similar issues, *individuals* can find comfort and realize that they are not alone in their experiences.

Hearing stories of triumph over adversity can provide a sense of hope and motivation, creating the belief that recovery is possible.

Insights from different perspectives

When celebrating progress, it is important to include a wide range of perspectives. Every individual's journey is unique, and by showcasing a variety of stories we can provide a more comprehensive understanding of resilience and empowerment. Perspectives from individuals of different ages, backgrounds and identities can shed light on the different ways people navigate their *mental health journeys*.

The role of *support systems*

Support systems play a crucial role in an individual's *mental health* journey. Whether it's family, friends, therapists, or support groups, having a strong network of people who believe in and support *one's progress is crucial*. Sharing stories that highlight the impact of these support systems can help individuals understand the importance of seeking and maintaining *strong connections*.

Overcoming obstacles: strategies for resilience

Resilience is not an innate quality; it can be cultivated and strengthened. Sharing stories that delve deeper into the strategies individuals have used to overcome obstacles can provide valuable insights and tools for others in their own *mental health* care. These strategies may include therapy, self-care practices, mindfulness techniques, or even lifestyle changes. By exploring a range of options, individuals can identify what works best for them and tailor their own resilience strategies.

Inspiring change: advocacy and activism

In addition to personal stories, celebrating progress also includes recognizing the power of mental health advocacy and activism. Many people who have faced mental health challenges become passionate advocates, working to raise awareness, challenge stigma, and improve access to care. Highlighting these stories can inspire others to become agents of change within their own communities and contribute to a society that values and supports *mental wellness*.

The journey continues: embracing growth

Finally, it is important to emphasize that celebrating progress is not the end of the journey. Mental health is a lifelong process, and growth and adversity are both integral parts of it. By sharing stories that recognize the ongoing nature of *mental health*, we can inspire individuals to embrace their own growth and continue to seek support and empowerment *throughout their lives.*

Celebrating progress through stories of resilience and empowerment is a powerful way to promote FTM mental health. By sharing personal stories, providing diverse perspectives, highlighting the role of support systems, exploring strategies for resilience, inspiring change through advocacy, and embracing continuous growth , we can foster a sense of community, break the stigma surrounding *mental health* , and empowering individuals. Their own journeys.

CHAPTER SIXTEEN

The importance of inner peace in stressful situations.

In our fast-paced world, stress is an inevitable part of our lives. Whether it's the pressure to meet deadlines, the stress of dealing with difficult people, or the anxiety caused by unexpected events, stress is something we all deal with on a regular basis. In such situations, finding inner peace is crucial as it helps us stay calm, focused and in control. *Inner peace* is not just a state of mind, but a way of life that can help us deal with stress and anxiety in *a healthier way , and it can have a profound impact* on *our overall well-being* .

Here are some insights about the importance of inner peace in *stressful situations* that you may find helpful:

Inner peace helps reduce stress levels:

When we feel stressed, our body releases a hormone called cortisol, which can negatively impact our health if it remains high for long periods of time. Inner peace can help lower cortisol levels in our bodies, reducing the harmful effects of stress on our physical and mental health.

Inner peace helps improve our mental health:

When we are stressed, our mind can become overwhelmed with negative thoughts and emotions, leading to anxiety and depression. Inner peace can help calm our minds and promote positive thinking, which can improve our mental health and well-being.

Inner peace helps improve our relationships:

Stressful situations can often lead to conflict and misunderstandings in our relationships with others. Inner peace can help us communicate more effectively, understand others better, and promote *healthier relationships.*

Inner peace helps us make better decisions:

When we are stressed, we are more likely to make impulsive decisions that we may later regret. Inner peace can **help us stay calm and focused**, allowing us to make *better decisions* that better align with our values and goals.

Finding inner peace is essential for our well-being, especially in stressful situations. By cultivating inner peace , we can reduce stress levels, improve our mental health, build healthier relationships, and make better decisions. So take a moment to breathe, relax, and find your *inner peace, even in the midst of the chaos.*

CHAPTER SEVENTEEN

The Mental Health Benefits of Road Trips.

The benefits of road trips for *mental health*

Road trips are often associated with adventure, excitement and freedom. However, the benefits of road trips go beyond just the thrill of the open road. Road trips can also have a positive impact on our mental health. In this section, we explore the different ways road trips can benefit our mental well-being .

1. Reduce stress and anxiety

One of the main benefits of road trips is its ability to reduce stress and anxiety. When we embark on a road trip, we leave our daily routine behind and enter a new environment. This change of scenery can help us disconnect from the stressors of our daily lives and give us a sense of freedom. Additionally, road trips allow us to do activities that we might not have time for during our normal routine, such as hiking, sightseeing, or simply enjoying the scenery. These activities can be therapeutic and help us relax and unwind.

2. **Promote mindfulness**

Road trips offer the opportunity to be present in the moment and practice mindfulness. When we're on the road, we're forced to slow down and appreciate our surroundings. We can enjoy the beauty of nature, enjoy the company of our travel companions and be fully present in the moment. This mindfulness practice can help us reduce stress and improve *our mental well-being.*

3. **Stimulate creativity**

Road trips can also stimulate our creativity. When we are in a new environment, we are exposed to different sights, sounds and experiences. This exposure can boost our creativity and **inspire us to think outside the box** . Plus, road trips provide the opportunity to do activities that we might not have time for during our normal routine, such as writing, painting or photography. These creative outlets can be therapeutic and help us express ourselves in *new ways.*

4. **Improve relationships**

Road trips can also improve our relationships with others. When we travel with others, we have the opportunity to share shared experiences and create lasting memories. Additionally, road trips provide the opportunity to disconnect from technology and social media and engage in *meaningful conversations.* This quality time with loved ones can help us feel more connected and improve *our mental well-being.*

Road trips can have a significant impact on our mental health. They offer the opportunity to reduce stress and anxiety, promote mindfulness, stimulate creativity and improve relationships. When planning a road trip, it's important to prioritize activities that benefit our mental well-being and make sure we take the time to practice self-care. Whether we travel alone or with others, road trips can be a powerful tool for improving our mental health and well-being .

CHAPTER EIGHTEEN

Meet the Startup Game Changers: Wearable Technology: Mental Health Monitoring and Management .

Monitor mood and emotions

Wearable technology has revolutionized the way we monitor and manage our mental health. Using advanced sensors and data analytics, these devices can track and analyze various aspects of our well-being, including our mood and emotions. For people struggling with mental health issues such as depression or anxiety, wearable devices can provide valuable insights into *their emotional state* and help them better understand their triggers and patterns.

For example, the Muse headband is a wearable device that uses electroencephalography (EEG) technology to measure brain wave activity. By wearing this device, *individuals* can get real-time feedback on their brain activity and learn to recognize and regulate their emotions. This can be especially beneficial for people with conditions such as *bipolar disorder*, where mood swings can be intense and unpredictable.

Stress reduction and relaxation techniques

Wearable technology can also be used to promote relaxation and reduce stress levels, which are crucial factors in maintaining *good mental health*. Devices like the Spire Stone are intended to detect and manage stress by monitoring breathing patterns. By measuring the user's breathing rate and providing real-time feedback, the device helps individuals become aware of their stress levels and encourages them to engage in *deep breathing exercises* or other relaxation techniques.

Another example is the Thync Relax Pro, a wearable device that uses neurostimulation technology to stimulate specific nerves in the head and neck. This device claims to induce a state of calm and relaxation by delivering gentle electrical pulses. By using wearable technology to promote relaxation, individuals can effectively manage stress and improve *their overall mental well-being*.

Sleep monitoring and optimization

Sleep plays a crucial role in mental health, and *wearable technology* can provide *valuable insights* into our sleep patterns and quality. Devices such as the Fitbit Sense or the Oura Ring are equipped with advanced sleep tracking features that monitor factors such as sleep duration, sleep stages and heart rate variability during sleep. By analyzing this data, individuals can identify *any problems* with their sleep and make *the necessary adjustments* to improve their sleep quality.

For example, if someone with anxiety notices consistently poor sleep quality; he or she can use this information to develop a bedtime routine that includes relaxation techniques or other strategies to promote better sleep. By using wearable technology to monitor and optimize sleep, individuals can address potential sleep-related issues and improve their mental health.

In short, wearable technology has opened up a world of possibilities for monitoring and managing mental health. From tracking mood and emotions to promoting relaxation and optimizing sleep, these innovative devices provide individuals with valuable insights and tools to take control of their mental well-being. As technology continues to develop, we can expect even more exciting developments in this area, further increasing our ability to support and improve mental health.

CHAPTER NINETEEN

How this affects our lives.

Regret is something we all experience at some point in our lives. It is that feeling of disappointment and sadness that occurs when we reflect on past choices that we wish we had made differently. Although regret is a powerful motivator for change can be, it can also be incredibly harmful if we allow it to consume us. The high cost of regret can affect our lives in many ways, from our *mental health* to our relationships and even our physical well-being. In this section we will explore *some of the ways* in which Regret can impact our lives and provide *some strategies* for minimizing *its effects*.

1. **Regret and Mental Health:** Studies have shown that regret can have a significant impact on our mental health. People who experience high levels of regret are more likely to

suffer from depression, anxiety and other mental health disorders. One reason for this is that regret often involves dwelling on the past, which can lead to feelings of hopelessness and helplessness. To minimize the impact of regret on our *mental health*, it is important to focus on the present and future rather than on to remain the past.

2. **Regrets and Relationships:** Regrets can also have *a significant impact* on our relationships. When we regret past choices, we may feel guilty or ashamed, which can lead to a breakdown in communication and trust with our loved ones. It is important to be open and honest with our partners and friends about our regrets, but also to forgive ourselves and move forward.

3. **Regret and *Physical Health*** : Believe it or not, regret can also have an impact on our *physical health* . Studies have shown that people who experience high levels of regret are more likely to suffer from chronic stress, which can lead to a range of health problems , including heart disease, diabetes, and obesity. To minimize the impact of regret on our *physical health, it's important to find healthy ways* to manage stress, such as exercise, meditation, or talking to a therapist.

Although regret is a natural and unavoidable part of life, it is important to be aware of its potential impact on our lives. By focusing on the present and future, being open and honest with our loved ones and *healthy manners* By finding ways to manage stress, we can minimize the high costs of regret and live happier, healthier lives.

CHAPTER TWEENTY

What lies ahead for behavioral health crowdfunding .

Crowdfunding has become a powerful tool to address various societal challenges , and behavioral health is no exception. As we delve into the future prospects of crowdfunding in behavioral health, it is essential to recognize the nuanced landscape shaping this innovative approach to *mental health* support. Let's take a look at the multi-faceted aspects, *potential benefits* and challenges that await us:

1. *Increased accessibility* and reach:

- Behavioral health crowdfunding platforms have the potential to democratize access to *mental health* resources. By allowing individuals to contribute directly to *specific causes* or campaigns, these platforms bridge gaps in traditional healthcare systems.

- Example: A young person struggling with anxiety may find solace in a crowdfunding campaign that aims to provide free counseling services. The ability to donate even a small amount can collectively make *a significant impact.*

2. **Tailor -made solutions and personalization** :

- In contrast to one-size-fits-all approaches, crowdfunding enables tailor-made interventions. Donors can choose projects that align with their values, whether supporting research, community programs or *individual therapy sessions* .

- Example: A donor passionate about destigmatizing mental health in schools could fund an anti-bullying campaign that includes workshops and awareness campaigns.

3. **Innovation and research financing** :

- Crowdfunding in behavioral health can accelerate research and innovation. Researchers, doctors and startups can present their ideas directly to the public, bypassing *bureaucratic hurdles* .

- Example: A team of psychologists who want to develop a mobile app for anxiety management can raise money through a crowdfunding campaign . This **app could revolutionize** self-help strategies.

4. **Community Building and Advocacy** :

- Crowdfunding campaigns promote a sense of community. Contributors become advocates, spreading awareness and encouraging others to participate.

- Example: A nonprofit organization focused on suicide prevention could host an annual crowdfunding event. Donors not only contribute financially, but also attend workshops and participate in discussions.

5. *Ethical considerations* **and transparency** :

- As behavioral health crowdfunding grows, *ethical questions* arise . How do we ensure transparency? What happens if a campaign does not achieve its objectives?

- Example: A campaign to provide therapy to trauma survivors must communicate transparently how the funds will be used. *Regular updates* and accountability are crucial.

6. **Dealing with concerns about stigma and privacy** :

- Some people hesitate to seek *mental health care* due to stigma. Crowd funding campaigns must balance privacy with the need for visibility.

- Example: A campaign to support the mental health of LGBTQ+ youth should respect the privacy of participants while emphasizing the importance of destigmatization.

7. **Integration with *existing systems*** :

- The future lies in integrating crowd funding with established *mental health* services. Collaboration between platforms, non-profit organizations and healthcare providers can increase the impact.

- Example: a hospital partners with a crowdfunding platform to raise money for a new *mental health* wing . Donors receive updates on patient results and *ongoing research*.

In summary, crowdfunding in behavioral health holds enormous promise. However, it requires thoughtful navigation, ethical guidelines and a commitment to transparency. As we move forward, let's harness its potential to strengthen mental health and create *a more compassionate world*.